The Magic School Bus
Inside a Beehive

The Magic School Bus
Inside a Beehive

By Joanna Cole / Illustrated by Bruce Degen

Scholastic Inc.

New York · Toronto · London · Auckland · Sydney
Mexico City · New Delhi · Hong Kong · Buenos Aires

The author and illustrator wish to thank Professor Mark L. Winston, Department of Biological Sciences,
Simon Fraser University, British Columbia, Canada, for his assistance in preparing this book.

For their helpful advice and consultation, thanks also to Ray Pupedis,
Division of Entomology, Yale-Peabody Museum of Natural History, New Haven, Connecticut;
Eric H. Erickson, Center Director, Carl Hayden Bee Research Center, Tuscon, Arizona;
and Mark Richardson, who kindly gave us a tour of his beehive.

ISBN-13: 978-0-590-25721-3
ISBN-10: 0-590-25721-8

60 59 58 57   19/0

Printed in the U.S.A.   40

The illustrator used pen and ink, watercolor, color pencil,
and gouache for the paintings in this book.

To my
honey, Phil.

J.C.

To
Will Tressler
and Jim Setz, and
all the busy bees who
are building our new hive.

B.D.

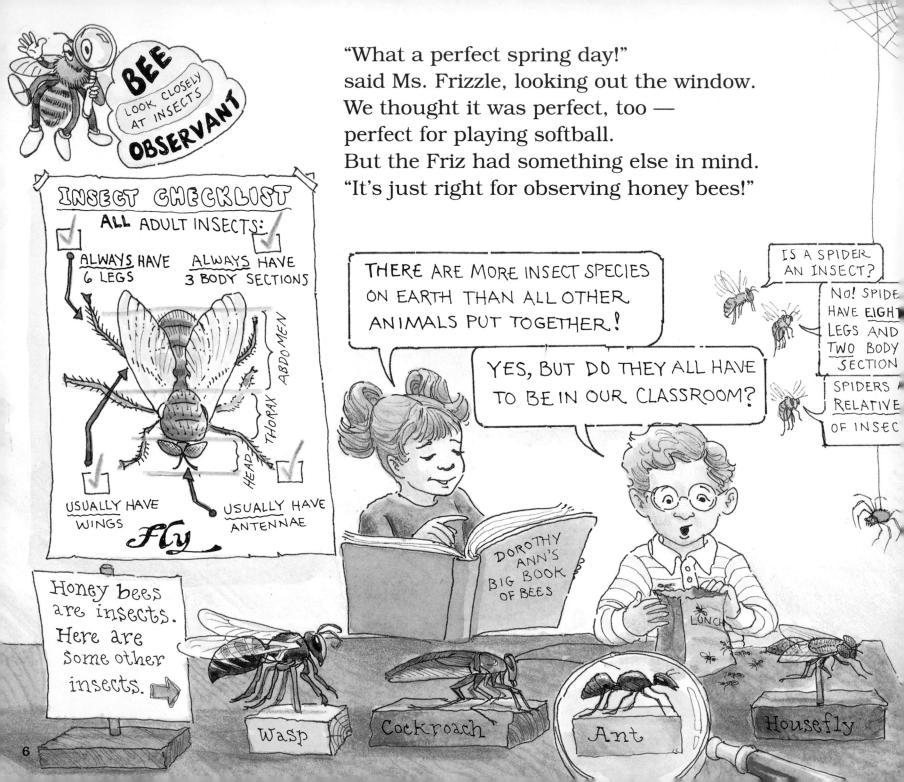

"What a perfect spring day!"
said Ms. Frizzle, looking out the window.
We thought it was perfect, too —
perfect for playing softball.
But the Friz had something else in mind.
"It's just right for observing honey bees!"

We had been studying about all different kinds of insects.
Now Ms. Frizzle said she had found a beekeeper who would show us his honey bee hives.

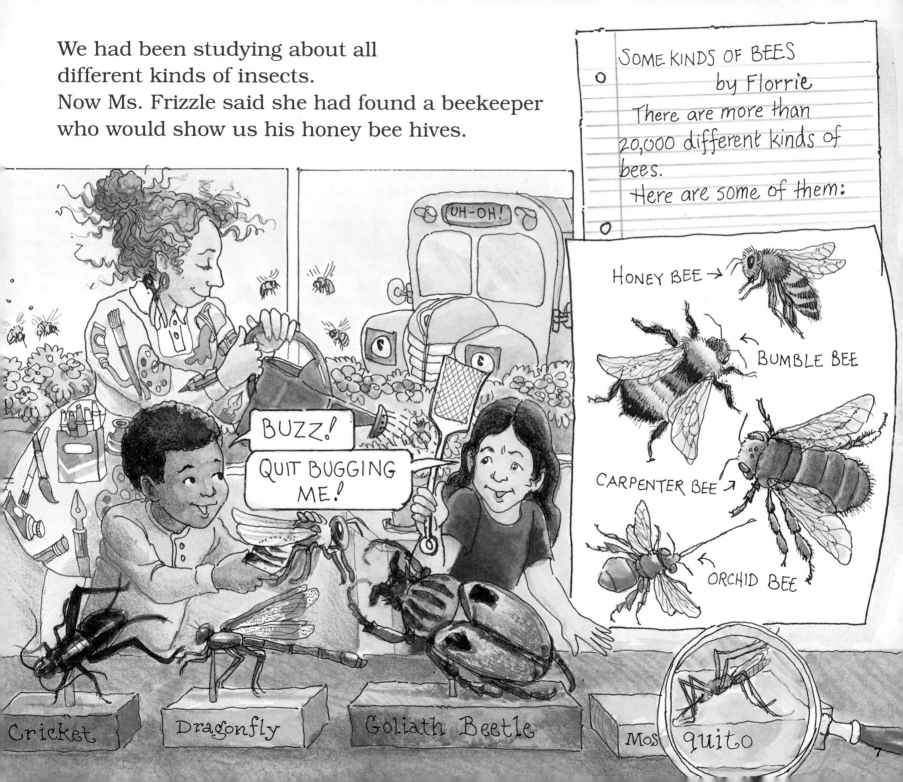

SOME KINDS OF BEES
by Florrie
There are more than 20,000 different kinds of bees.
Here are some of them:

HONEY BEE →

BUMBLE BEE

CARPENTER BEE →

ORCHID BEE

UH-OH!

BUZZ!

QUIT BUGGING ME!

Cricket

Dragonfly

Goliath Beetle

Mosquito

7

"The beekeeper is visiting his hives today. We'll meet him there," said the Friz, and she swept out the door.

As we boarded the old school bus,
Ms. Frizzle talked and talked
about honey bees.
"They make a delicious food
for us to eat," she said.
"They help many plants survive.
And they are wonderful examples
of social insects!"

BEES ARE MY FAVORITE INSECTS.

WHAT IS <u>YOUR</u> FAVORITE INSECT, ARNOLD?

...I'M NOT THE KIND OF PERSON WHO HAS A FAVORITE INSECT.

WHAT ARE SOCIAL INSECTS?
by Wanda
Social insects live and work together in a community.
Some social insects:

<u>Ants</u> nest in the ground.

<u>Paper</u> <u>wasps</u> make a nest out of wood pulp.

<u>Bumble</u> <u>bees</u> nest in grass-lined holes in the ground.

Termites nest in wood.

A WORD FROM DOROTHY ANN
Social comes from a word that means "friend" or "partner."

9

WHY DO BEES STING?
by Phoebe

Stinging is the way bees protect their hive.
Bees usually sting only if they have to. That's because they die soon after they sting.

> I'LL STING, BUT ONLY FOR A GOOD CAUSE...

> ...SUCH AS SAVING THE HIVE.

Honey bees have barbs, or hooks, on the end of their stingers.

STINGER   BARB

When a honey bee stings, her stinger gets stuck in the victim's skin. The stinger is pulled out of the bee's body, and the bee **dies**.

Ms. Frizzle drove out into the country and parked the bus next to the hives. The beekeeper was late, so Frizzie took out a picnic basket. "Some light refreshments will pass the time while we wait," she said. Sometimes, our teacher has *good* ideas!

BEE AROUND STINGING INSECT. CAREFUL

> BEES USUALLY WILL NOT STING, UNLESS YOU TOUCH THEM, ANNOY THEM, OR GET TOO CLOSE TO THEIR HIVE.

> MAY WE CLOSE THE WINDOWS, PLEASE?

HONEY

But just as she opened
a jar of honey,
her elbow knocked
a strange little lever.
The honey jar fell, and
we heard a weird
buzzing sound.

It was the bus.
It was vibrating,
and getting smaller.
So was everything in it —
including *us!*

BEEHIVES THROUGH THE AGES
by Tim
Wild bees have always made their homes in hollow trees or logs.
Human-made hives are built of straw, pottery, or wood.

Straw

Wood

Pottery

Tree

MEANWHILE

UH-OH!

BOB'S BETTER BEES

COMING FROM THE WEST

Before we knew it, the bus looked like a little beehive, and we looked like real bees! We really did!
"All out, class," buzzed the Friz.

BE A BEE, EVERYONE!

DO WE HAVE A CHOICE?

STOP POKING ME WITH YOUR ANTENNAE!

STOP STEPPING ON MY WING!

THESE THINGS DON'T HAPPEN ON MOST CLASS TRIPS.

One by one, we stepped out the door and looked over at the nearest hive. At the entrance, worker bees were standing guard. "Guard bees usually keep out bees from other hives," said the Friz.

ENTRANCE

GUARD BEE IN POSITION TO MEET INCOMING BEES

ACCORDING TO MY RESEARCH, GUARD BEES WILL BITE AND STING STRANGE BEES.

DO WE QUALIFY AS "STRANGE BEES"?

NO DOUBT ABOUT IT!

DOROTHY ANN'S BIG BOOK OF BEES

"We'll have to visit flowers and get bee food in order to gain entrance to the hive. Follow that bee!" shouted the Friz. We flew after a bee that was headed toward some bright flowers.

MEANWHILE

COMING FROM THE EAST

EXACTLY WHAT DOES SHE MEAN BY "GAIN ENTRANCE TO THE HIVE"?

SHE MEANS GO INSIDE IT.

I WAS AFRAID OF THAT...

FLYING IS FUN!

BUZZ OFF!

BEES HELP FLOWERS MAKE SEEDS

by Alex

As bees visit flowers, they <u>pollinate</u> them. This means they carry pollen from one flower to another.

Pollen
Pollen tube
Fertilized egg
Ovary
Honey stomach (inside body)
Tongue
Nectar

When a grain of pollen joins with an egg cell in a flower, a seed begins to grow.

MANY PLANTS CANNOT MAKE SEEDS UNLESS BEES POLLINATE THEIR FLOWERS.

WE NEED BEES!

"Observe our bee, children, and do exactly what she does!" Ms. Frizzle called.
The bee stuck her long tubelike tongue deep into a flower and pumped out nectar.
We each did the same with a rubber tube.
"The bee carries the nectar in a pouch called the honey stomach," Frizzie told us.
We carried our nectar in a tiny bottle.

BEE POLLINATE THEM! KIND TO FLOWERS

BE A BEE! COLLECT NECTAR AND POLLEN.

Pollen grains rubbed off the flower
and stuck onto the bee's "fur."
With her front and middle legs,
she combed off the pollen and packed it
into pollen baskets —
pouches on her back legs.
Then she returned to the hive.
We packed our pollen and went along.

BEES HELP MAKE FOOD FOR PEOPLE
by John
Bees pollinate many crop plants-- plants that give us our food.

Apple

Blueberry

Squash

Orange

AT MY OLD SCHOOL, WE NEVER COLLECTED FLOWER PRODUCTS.

IF WE HAVE A LOT, MAYBE THE BEES WON'T STING US.

I'M GETTING EXTRA!

POLLEN BASKET

POLLEN BASKET

WE NEED BEES!

BEES "TALK" WITH SMELLS!
by Amanda Jane

PHEROMONES are body chemicals that allow animals to "talk" to each other by smell.

> WHEW! DO YOU HAVE TO "TALK" SO LOUD?

With pheromones, bees send each other many messages. Here are some of them:

"I'm a hive-mate."
"I'm a stranger."
"I'm a worker."
"I'm the queen bee!"
"Danger! Danger!"
"Defend the hive!"

Bees don't talk in words, but they do communicate.

One by one, we landed at the hive.
The Friz sprayed us with a bee pheromone —
a chemical that bees make.
Now we smelled like bees.
Then came the scary part.

> THERE MAY BE AS MANY AS 60,000 BEES IN ONE HIVE, CLASS.

> WHAT IF THEY NOTICE WE'RE NOT REAL BEES?

> SPRAY ME AGAIN PLEASE, MS. FRIZZLE!

> BEE BRAVE KIDS!

> BE A BEE

We held our breath as the guard bees brushed us with their antennae, smelling us. If they fell for our trick, we'd get into the hive. If they didn't, we'd get into big trouble!

WE'RE TAKING A BIG CHANCE.

I'LL BUZZ TO THAT!

WORK ORDERS

☑ Guard entrance
☑ Clean hive
☑ Build comb
☑ Make honey
☑ Fan wings to cool hive
☑ Tend queen
☑ Feed baby bees
☑ Collect pollen and nectar

WHO'S WHO IN THE HIVE?
by Michael

In a honey bee colony, there are three castes, or kinds, of bees:

1. The QUEEN: Her job is to lay eggs, eggs, and more eggs!

QUEEN

2. The WORKERS: They are all female bees that usually do not lay eggs. Workers do almost all the jobs in the hive.

3. The DRONES are all male bees. A male bee's only job is to mate with a queen.

WORKER   DRONE

19

A BEEHIVE COMES IN SECTIONS
by Molly

- TOP
- INSIDE COVER
- "SUPER" FRAMES (HOLD THE EXTRA HONEY WE TAKE TO EAT)
- QUEEN EXCLUDER (KEEPS QUEEN IN LOWER SECTIONS)
- FRAME WITH COMB
- CELLS (HOLD BABY BEES, HONEY, AND POLLEN)
- DEEP HIVE BOX
- ENTRANCE
- LANDING PLATFORM

WE ARE HERE

The guards smelled our bee spray and our bee food. They let us pass! Other workers took our nectar and bustled off with it.
"Hooray! We're free to explore the hive!" sang out Ms. Frizzle.

MEANWHILE

WATER

BOB'S BETTER BEES

COMING FROM THE WEST

The first thing we saw was our bee.
She was doing a strange dance.
Other bees crowded around her,
touching her and listening to her.
Ms. Frizzle said the dance was a "language."
With her dance, the bee "told" others
which way to go to the flowers
she had found.

OUR BEE

MEANWHILE

SNIFF SNIFF

COMING FROM THE EAST

THE ROUND DANCE
by Phil
This dance tells bees that a food source is close to the hive. The dancing bee walks in a circle, then turns around and goes the other way.

The other bees go outside and fly in a circular pattern near the hive until they find the flowers.

BEE-HIVE

22

The dance helped the bees find food faster. They did not have to waste time looking for it. They flew off in the direction of the flowers we had visited.

BEES HAVE MANY DANCES.

EACH DANCE "SAYS" SOMETHING DIFFERENT.

DOROTHY ANN'S BIG BOOK OF BEES

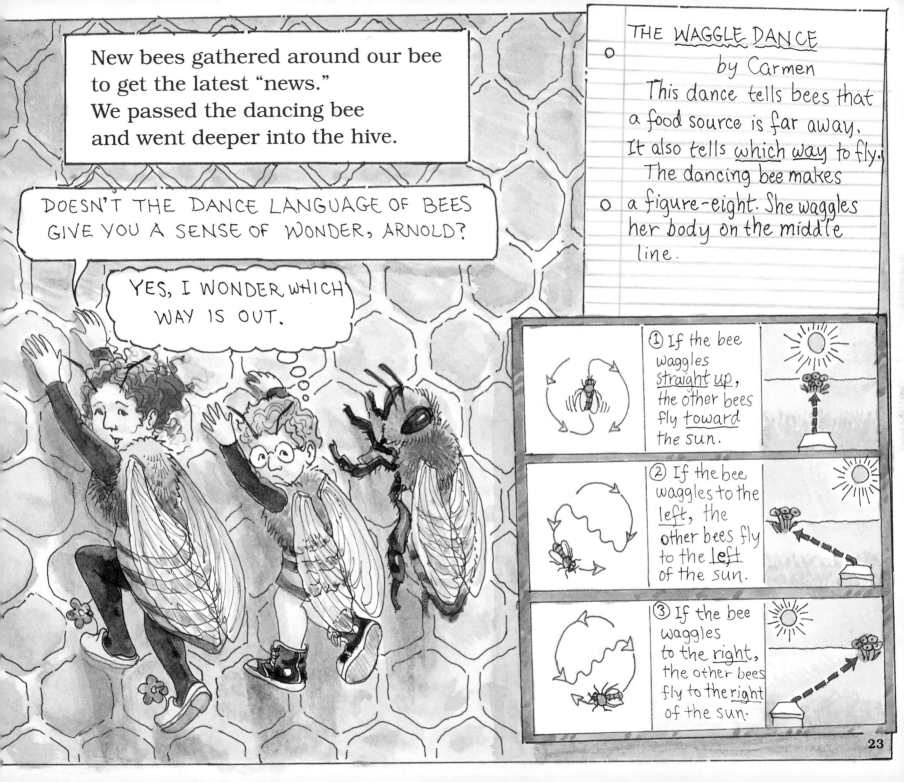

New bees gathered around our bee to get the latest "news." We passed the dancing bee and went deeper into the hive.

DOESN'T THE DANCE LANGUAGE OF BEES GIVE YOU A SENSE OF WONDER, ARNOLD?

YES, I WONDER WHICH WAY IS OUT.

THE WAGGLE DANCE
by Carmen
This dance tells bees that a food source is far away. It also tells which way to fly. The dancing bee makes a figure-eight. She waggles her body on the middle line.

① If the bee waggles straight up, the other bees fly toward the sun.

② If the bee waggles to the left, the other bees fly to the left of the sun.

③ If the bee waggles to the right, the other bees fly to the right of the sun.

LOOK INSIDE ME.

WAX GLANDS

LOOK UNDERNEATH ME.

OPENINGS FOR WAX

FRAME WITH COMB

HONEY   HONEY

POLLEN

EGGS AND LARVAE

PUPAE
(CAPPED CELLS)

WE ARE HERE

DEEP HIVE BOX

24

The inside of the hive was covered with beeswax.
The bees had shaped the wax into comb —
thousands of little containers called cells.
Every cell was a hexagon — a six-sided shape.
The comb was so perfect,
we couldn't believe bees had made it.
"Make comb, class!" said Ms. Frizzle.

ALMOST ALL BEE LIFE TAKES PLACE ON THE COMB, CLASS.

BEES DANCE ON THE COMB.

THEY WALK AND REST ON THE COMB.

BEE MAKE HEXAGONS HELPFUL

We did our best, but our cells
came out pretty lopsided.
Luckily, the bees didn't notice us.
They just tore down our cells
and built them over again.
Other bees were busy with other jobs,
such as making honey.

BEES RAISE BABIES IN THE COMB CELLS.

THEY STORE NECTAR AND POLLEN IN THE CELLS.

THEY MAKE HONEY IN THE CELLS, TOO.

THAT'S SWEET OF THEM.

HOW BEES MAKE COMB
by Rachel

A bee uses her back and middle legs to pass wax to her front legs.
Then she chews and shapes the wax into cells.

Honey bees make the comb cells tilt up so the honey doesn't drip out!

HONEY
POLLEN

25

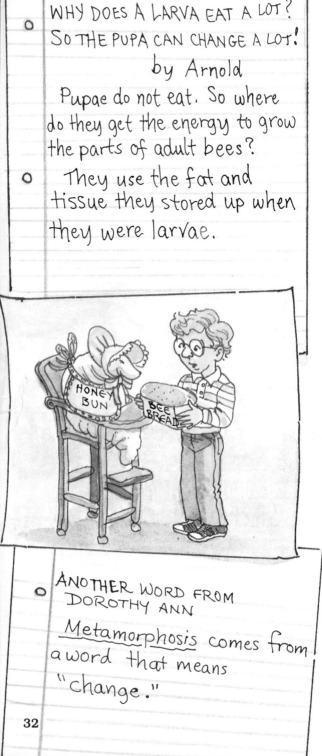

WHY DOES A LARVA EAT A LOT?
SO THE PUPA CAN CHANGE A LOT!
by Arnold

Pupae do not eat. So where do they get the energy to grow the parts of adult bees?

They use the fat and tissue they stored up when they were larvae.

ANOTHER WORD FROM DOROTHY ANN

Metamorphosis comes from a word that means "change."

32

"When it is big enough, the larva stops eating," said the Friz. "It spins a silk cocoon around itself. Now it is called a pupa.
The nurse bees put a wax top on the cell.
Inside, the pupa doesn't eat or grow bigger.
It changes into an adult bee.
This is called metamorphosis.

"When the pupae have finished
changing into adult bees,
they chew their way out of their cells,"
continued Ms. Frizzle.
We saw new worker bees emerging.
They let the air dry them off
and started working right away.
Meanwhile, we heard excited buzzing.
What was happening?

BEE

GROW UP!

ADULT

NOW THE METAMORPHOSIS IS COMPLETE, CHILDREN.

THE BEES ARE ALL GROWN UP.

I'M SO PROUD OF THEM.

THE ROAD FROM **EGG** TO **BEE**

EGG LARVA PUPA ADULT

SWARMING BEES USUALLY DON'T STING
by Phoebe

Usually bees sting because they have a hive to protect. A swarm does not. It's a colony of bees that's "between hives."

WE'RE LOOKING FOR AN EMPTY BEEHIVE...

...OR A NICE HOLLOW TREE.

SWARM

MEANWHILE

THE BEAR FINDS THE HIVE

The queen was leaving the hive! And she was taking almost half the workers with her! They flew away in a thick swarm. What would become of the hive now?

EXIT

SWARMING IS NATURE'S WAY OF STARTING NEW BEEHIVES.

BUT HOW CAN THE OLD HIVE SURVIVE WITHOUT THE QUEEN?

THERE'S NO ONE TO LAY EGGS NOW.

DON'T BE SO SURE. REMEMBER THE QUEEN CELLS?

Ms. Frizzle led the way to the queen cells. Two new queens emerged at the same time.

After they had dried out, they had a terrible fight. One queen stung the other queen to death!

Then she killed the other queen pupae in their cells. Now she was the new queen.

TWO QUEENS? I THOUGHT...

THERE WAS ONLY...

ONE QUEEN IN A HIVE.

A QUEEN BEE CAN STING MANY TIMES   by Arnold
Unlike worker bees, which can sting only once, the queen bee can pull her stinger out of the victim and sting again.

YOU WERE ABSOLUTELY RIGHT.

THE STRONGER QUEEN SURVIVES TO PASS ON HER STRENGTH TO HER CHILDREN.

35

After the new queen left,
we heard heavy footsteps.
It was a bear, trying to steal the honey
and the bee larvae!
The workers flew out and tried to sting the bear,
but its thick fur protected its body.

MEANWHILE

BEEKEEPER STILL ON THE WAY

IF THE BEAR BREAKS OPEN THE HIVE...

AND EATS ALL THE HONEY AND THE LARVAE...

THE BEES MAY NOT SURVIVE!

WE HAVE TO HELP!

STING HIM!

I CAN'T GET THROUGH!

HELP!

COMMON HIVE RAIDERS
by Tim

Skunks

Bears

Wasps

Bees from
other hives

Bees can defeat most robbers, but bears are hard to beat.

BEWARE
NEVER GET CLOSE TO BEARS. THEY MAY LOOK CUTE, BUT THEY ARE VERY DANGEROUS.

We flew out and dived at the bear, but it kept coming at the hive. "We have to use strategy, class," called the Friz. "We'll lure the bear away!"

BEE FOR ANYTHING PREPARE

BE A BEE! DEFEND THE HIVE!

BUT I DON'T WANT TO HURT A CUTE LITTLE BEAR.

I WOULDN'T SAY CUTE AND LITTLE.

I'D SAY BIG AND HUNGRY!

Ms. Frizzle made a beeline for the beehive-bus —
and we followed.
The jar of honey that had spilled before was
still on the floor.
The bear smelled the honey and came after us.
"Ms. Frizzle!" we yelled. "Do something!"
She stepped on the gas, and the bus lurched forward.

THE BEAR WILL
FOLLOW OUR
HONEY AWAY
FROM THE HIVE,
CLASS.

MS. FRIZZLE SPILLED
THAT HONEY BEFORE
WE CHANGED INTO
BEES...

AND BEFORE WE
BECAME BEAR BAIT.

THOSE WERE THE
GOOD OLD DAYS.

UN-BEARABLE

As we rounded a corner,
the honey jar rolled out the bus door.
As the jar fell, it returned to its normal size.
The bear started eating honey and forgot all about us.

40

Ms. Frizzle reached for a joystick
on the dashboard.
To our relief, the bus lifted off.
It wasn't a beehive-bus anymore. It was a bee-bus!
Down below, we saw the new queen returning home
from her nuptial flight.

THE HIVE IS SAFE!

WE'RE SAFE!

WE'LL MEET THE BEEKEEPER
ANOTHER DAY, CLASS. RIGHT
NOW, WE'RE RETURNING TO
THE CLASSROOM.

IT'S ABOUT TIME

We returned home from our flight, too.
The instant its six feet touched the ground
in the school parking lot, the bee-bus changed.

It was a full-size school bus again.
We were human kids again.

BUSY BEE RIDDLES

Q: Why do bees itch?
A: They have hives.

Q: Why did the bee hum at her singing lesson?
A: She didn't know the words.

Q: How does a bee fix her hair?
A: She uses a honey comb.

Q: What grade did the students get on their honey project?
A: They all got B's!

REPORT CARD
B

And back in the classroom, we thought of the perfect project to end the day: baking honey buns, of course!

I KIND OF MISS BEING A BEE.

YES, I FEEL LOST WITHOUT MY ANTENNAE.

I LIKED THE STRIPES.

THE BEST PART WAS THE HONEY... AND WE CAN STILL GET THAT FROM BEEKEEPERS!

BYE-BYE BEES

To: Ms. Frizzle and her class

BOB'S BETTER BEES

HONEY FROM BOB'S BEEHIVE

HONEY FROM BOB'S BEEHIVE

44

45

47